A TRAVELER'S PRAYER BOOK

CHRISTOPHER L. WEBBER

SEABURY BOOKS

an imprint of

CHURCH PUBLISHING, NEW YORK

Church Publishing Incorporated
445 Fifth Avenue
New York, NY 10016

5   4   3   2   1

Contents

Introduction

*W*e travel for many reasons: business, pleasure, and family occasions among them. And when we travel, we leave behind our accustomed pattern of life. Our routine is disrupted and each day we find ourselves adapting to unfamiliar places and schedules. But, regardless of these superficial distractions, we continue to need regular times of prayer.

Though we are absent from our own home and community, we are no further away from God. Setting aside regular times of prayer as we travel can help keep us "on track"—remind us who we are and what our life is for. As with almost every change, the disruption created by travel presents both an opportunity and a challenge. Human beings need a routine, but we also need to be pushed to see things in new ways. This book is designed to speak to both needs by offering a stable pattern of prayer and, at the same time, holding up the possibility of spiritual growth.

Surprisingly, a hotel or motel room can be a place to renew our spiritual life. Without all the material things that surround and distract us at home, time for prayer and meditation may be easier to find. Stimulated by the sights and sounds of a new place, we may be able to open our hearts and minds to God's presence.

I have culled the prayers in this book from a number of sources, including the Book of Common Prayer of the Episcopal Church, *Gates of the House: The New Union Prayerbook, A New Zealand Prayer Book,* and my own writings. The alternative forms for morning and evening prayer are based on *The Private Prayers* of Lancelot Andrewes. In general, I have cast the prayers in a personal mode, suitable for an individual traveling alone. However, they also lend themselves to group devotions.

I hope that the prayers and readings in this small book will provide a framework for your day, centering your thoughts around the presence of God, and offering stories about the ways in which other people on a journey have met with God.

May God guide you on your travels and bring you home at last to the love which always surrounds us.

Christopher L. Webber
Easter 1999

Prayers for the Start
of a Journey

Prayers for the Start of a Journey

These prayers may be read by a single traveler on an airplane, a train, a bus, or in a hotel room. They may be said by a group at home or at church. A Bible study group, a prayer group, or weekday service would be very appropriate settings. If several people are present, the psalms and canticles may be said responsively.

Lord, you trace my journeys and my resting-places
   you are acquainted with all my ways.

O God, you called Abraham and Sarah to leave
their home and protected them in all their
wanderings: Grant those who travel now by land,
sea, or air, a prosperous journey, a time of peace,
and a safe arrival at their journey's end. Be to
them a shadow in the heat, a refuge in the
tempest, a protection in adversity, and grant that
when life's pilgrimage is over they may arrive at
the heavenly country; through Jesus Christ our
Lord. Amen.

Psalm 139 (1–11, 22–23)

LORD, you have searched me out and known me; *
   you know my sitting down and my rising up;
   you discern my thoughts from afar.

You trace my journeys and my resting-places *
　　and are acquainted with all my ways.

Indeed, there is not a word on my lips, *
　　but you, O LORD, know it altogether.

You press upon me behind and before *
　　and lay your hand upon me.

Such knowledge is too wonderful for me; *
　　it is so high that I cannot attain to it.

Where can I go then from your Spirit? *
　　where can I flee from your presence?

If I climb up to heaven, you are there; *
　　if I make the grave my bed, you are there also.

If I take the wings of the morning *
　　and dwell in the uttermost parts of the sea,

Even there your hand will lead me *
　　and your right hand hold me fast.

If I say, "Surely the darkness will cover me, *
　　and the light around me turn to night,"

Darkness is not dark to you;
　　the night is as bright as the day; *
　　darkness and light to you are both alike.

Search me out, O God, and know my heart; *
  try me and know my restless thoughts.

Look well whether there be any wickedness in me *
  and lead me in the way that is everlasting.

↶

Lord, you trace my journeys and my resting-places
  you are acquainted with all my ways.

↶

Lord, have mercy.
  Christ, have mercy.
Lord, have mercy.

Our Father, who art in heaven,
  hallowed be thy Name,
  thy kingdom come,
  thy will be done,
      on earth as it is in heaven.
Give us this day our daily bread.
And forgive us our trespasses,
  as we forgive those
      who trespass against us.
And lead us not into temptation,
  but deliver us from evil.
For thine is the kingdom,
  and the power, and the glory,
  for ever and ever. Amen.

or this

Our Father in heaven,
   hallowed be your Name,
   your kingdom come,
   your will be done,
      on earth as in heaven.
Give us today our daily bread.
Forgive us our sins
   as we forgive those
      who sin against us.
Save us from the time of trial,
   and deliver us from evil.
For the kingdom, the power,
   and the glory are yours,
   now and for ever. Amen.

O God, save your servant
   Who puts *her* trust in you.
Be to *her* a strong tower
   Against every enemy.
Teach us your ways, O Lord,
   And we will walk in your truth.
Happy are they whose way is blameless,
   Who walk in the law of the Lord.
God shall give the angels charge over you
   To keep you in all your ways.

A highway shall be there,
  and it shall be called the Holy Way;
the unclean shall not travel on it,
  but it shall be for God's people;
no traveler, not even fools,
  shall go astray.
No lion shall be there,
  nor shall any ravenous beast come up on it;
they shall not be found there,
  but the redeemed shall walk there.
And the ransomed of the LORD shall return,
  and come to Zion with singing;
everlasting joy shall be upon their heads;
  they shall obtain joy and gladness,
and sorrow and sighing shall flee away. *(Isaiah 35:8–10)*

O God, our heavenly Father, whose glory fills the
whole creation, and whose presence we find
wherever we go: Preserve those who travel;
surround them with your loving care; protect
them from every danger; and bring them in safety
to their journey's end; through Jesus Christ our
Lord. Amen.

*M*ay the Lord watch over my going out and my
          coming in,
  from this time forth for evermore. Amen

Prayers while Traveling

To Begin the Day

Read these words from Psalm 51 (16, 11–13).

Open my lips, O Lord, *
  and my mouth shall proclaim your praise.
Create in me a clean heart, O God, *
  and renew a right spirit within me.
Cast me not away from your presence *
  and take not your holy Spirit from me.
Give me the joy of your saving help again *
  and sustain me with your bountiful Spirit.

Read this passage from the Bible, or one of the readings suggested on pages 49–97.

Blessed be the God and Father of our Lord Jesus Christ! By his great mercy he has given us a new birth into a living hope through the resurrection of Jesus Christ from the dead. *(1 Peter 1:3)*

Spend a few minutes (more if possible) quietly thinking about the passage you have read. See "Suggestions for Meditation," pages 43–45.

Pray for yourself and others. Use these prayers or others from pages 101–118.

Prayers for Guidance

*L*ord God, almighty and everlasting Father, you have brought us in safety to this new day: Preserve us with your mighty power, that we may not fall into sin, nor be overcome by adversity; and in all we do, direct us to the fulfilling of your purpose; through Jesus Christ our Lord. Amen.

*H*eavenly Father, in you we live and move and have our being: We humbly pray you so to guide and govern us by your Holy Spirit, that in all the cares and occupations of our life we may not forget you, but may remember that we are ever walking in your sight; through Jesus Christ our Lord. Amen.

*O*ur Father, who art in heaven,
   hallowed be thy Name,
   thy kingdom come,
   thy will be done,
      on earth as it is in heaven.
Give us this day our daily bread.

And forgive us our trespasses,
  as we forgive those
      who trespass against us.
And lead us not into temptation,
  but deliver us from evil.
For thine is the kingdom,
  and the power, and the glory,
  for ever and ever. Amen.

or this

Our Father in heaven,
  hallowed be your Name,
  your kingdom come,
  your will be done,
      on earth as in heaven.
Give us today our daily bread.
Forgive us our sins
  as we forgive those
      who sin against us.
Save us from the time of trial,
  and deliver us from evil.
For the kingdom, the power,
  and the glory are yours,
  now and for ever. Amen.

For the Middle of the Day

Read these words from Psalm 113 (1–4).

Give praise, you servants of the LORD; *
  praise the Name of the LORD.
Let the Name of the LORD be blessed, *
  from this time forth for evermore.
From the rising of the sun to its going down *
  let the Name of the LORD be praised.
The LORD is high above all nations, *
  and his glory above the heavens.

Read this passage from the Bible, or one of the readings suggested on pages 49–97.

Those of steadfast mind you keep in peace—
  in peace because they trust in you.

For thus said the Lord GOD, the Holy One of
      Israel:
In returning and rest you shall be saved;
in quietness and in trust shall be your strength.
(Isaiah 26:3, 30:15)

Spend a few minutes (more if possible) quietly thinking about the passage you have read. See "Suggestions for Meditation," pages 43–45.

Pray for yourself and others. Use these prayers or others from pages 101–118.

Blessed Savior, at this hour you hung upon the cross, stretching out your loving arms: Grant that all the peoples of the earth may look to you and be saved; for your tender mercies' sake. Amen.

Lord Jesus Christ, you said to your apostles, "Peace I give to you; my own peace I leave with you:" Regard not our sins, but the faith of your Church, and give to us the peace and unity of that heavenly City, where with the Father and the Holy Spirit you live and reign, now and for ever. Amen.

Our Father, who art in heaven,
    hallowed be thy Name,
    thy kingdom come,
    thy will be done,
        on earth as it is in heaven.
Give us this day our daily bread.
And forgive us our trespasses,
    as we forgive those
        who trespass against us.
And lead us not into temptation,
    but deliver us from evil.
For thine is the kingdom,
    and the power, and the glory,
    for ever and ever. Amen.

or this

Our Father in heaven,
   hallowed be your Name,
   your kingdom come,
   your will be done,
         on earth as in heaven.
Give us today our daily bread.
Forgive us our sins
   as we forgive those
         who sin against us.
Save us from the time of trial,
   and deliver us from evil.
For the kingdom, the power,
   and the glory are yours,
   now and for ever. Amen.

For the Early Evening

Read these words.

O gracious Light,
pure brightness of the everliving Father in heaven,
O Jesus Christ, holy and blessed!

Now as we come to the setting of the sun,
and our eyes behold the vesper light,
we sing your praises, O God: Father, Son, and
Holy Spirit.

You are worthy at all times to be praised by
happy voices,
O Son of God, O Giver of life,
and to be glorified through all the worlds.

Read this passage from the Bible, or one of the readings suggested on pages 49–97.

*W*e do not proclaim ourselves; we proclaim Jesus Christ as Lord and ourselves as your servants for Jesus' sake. For it is the God who said, "Let light shine out of darkness," who has shone in our hearts to give the light of the knowledge of the glory of God in the face of Jesus Christ.
(*2 Corinthians* 4:5–6)

Spend a few minutes (more if possible) quietly thinking about the passage you have read. See "Suggestions for Meditation," pages 43–45.

Pray for yourself and others. Use these prayers or others from pages 101–118.

*L*ord Jesus, stay with us, for evening is at hand and the day is past; be our companion in the way, kindle our hearts, and awaken hope, that we may know you as you are revealed in Scripture and the breaking of bread. Grant this for the sake of your love. Amen.

*O*ur Father, who art in heaven,
    hallowed be thy Name,
    thy kingdom come,
    thy will be done,
        on earth as it is in heaven.
Give us this day our daily bread.
And forgive us our trespasses,
    as we forgive those
        who trespass against us.
And lead us not into temptation,
    but deliver us from evil.
For thine is the kingdom,
    and the power, and the glory,
    for ever and ever. Amen.

or this

Our Father in heaven,
   hallowed be your Name,
   your kingdom come,
   your will be done,
       on earth as in heaven.
Give us today our daily bread.
Forgive us our sins
   as we forgive those
       who sin against us.
Save us from the time of trial,
   and deliver us from evil.
For the kingdom, the power,
   and the glory are yours,
   now and for ever. Amen.

For the End of the Day

Read Psalm 134.

*B*ehold now, bless the LORD, all you servants of
the LORD, *
you that stand by night in the house of the LORD.
Lift up your hands in the holy place and bless the
LORD; *
the LORD who made heaven and earth bless you
out of Zion.

*Read this passage from the Bible, or one of the readings suggested on
pages 49–97.*

*Y*et you, O LORD, are in the midst of us,
and we are called by your name; do not
forsake us!
O LORD our God.   *(Jeremiah 14:9,22)*

*L*ord, you now have set your servant free *
to go in peace as you have promised;
For these eyes of mine have seen the Savior, *
whom you have prepared for all the world to see:
A Light to enlighten the nations, *
and the glory of your people Israel.   *(Luke 2:29–32)*

Spend a few minutes (more if possible) quietly thinking about the passages you have read. See "Suggestions for Meditation," pages 43–45.

Pray for yourself and others. Use these prayers or others from pages 101–118.

Our Father, who art in heaven,
   hallowed be thy Name,
   thy kingdom come,
   thy will be done,
       on earth as it is in heaven.
Give us this day our daily bread.
And forgive us our trespasses,
   as we forgive those
       who trespass against us.
And lead us not into temptation,
   but deliver us from evil.
For thine is the kingdom,
   and the power, and the glory,
   for ever and ever. Amen.

or this

Our Father in heaven,
   hallowed be your Name,
   your kingdom come,
   your will be done,
       on earth as in heaven.
Give us today our daily bread.
Forgive us our sins
   as we forgive those
       who sin against us.

Save us from the time of trial,
   and deliver us from evil.
For the kingdom, the power,
   and the glory are yours,
      now and for ever. Amen.

*V*isit this place, O Lord, and drive far from it all snares of the enemy; let your holy angels dwell with us to preserve us in peace; and let your blessing be upon us always; through Jesus Christ our Lord. Amen.

*T*he almighty and merciful Lord, Father, Son, and Holy Spirit, bless us and keep us. Amen.

for the restoration of those
who have lost their faith;
for the strengthening of those
who have been given truth and grace;
for the comforting of those
who are depressed, in sickness, in trouble;
for thankfulness for all
who are healthy, prosperous, peaceful;

for the church in this country and throughout the
    world,
for its ministry,
for its members in their callings;
for the nations of the world;
for peace and justice in every place;
for the President of the United Sates,
for the Congress and the Courts;
for governors, mayors, and civil authority;
for police and firefighters;
for lawyers, judges, doctors, and nurses,
for farmers, merchants, and mechanics,
for teachers and students;
for those who will serve me this day as I eat and
    travel;

for those who are close to me
in my family,
in my work
and in my community;

for those who love me
though I may not know them or may have
    forgotten them;
for those who may hate me without a cause;
for all I have promised to remember in my prayers
and all who remember me in their prayers;
for all who have no one to pray for them;
for all who are at this moment in great need;
for all who are setting out this day
to serve you and to serve others
and to bring glory to the Name of God;
for all who act nobly
toward the church and toward the poor;
for all whom I have ever offended
either in word or in deed.

O God, have mercy on me and bless me,
lift up the light of your countenance upon me;
bless me and receive my prayer.
Direct my life toward your commandments,
hallow my soul,
purify my body,
correct my thoughts,
cleanse my desires,
my soul and body, my mind and spirit.
Renew me thoroughly, O God,
for in you I find my strength. Amen.

A longer form of Evening Prayer

This prayer should be said slowly and thoughtfully and filled out with the particular needs known to you.

'The day is gone,
and I give you thanks, O Lord.
Evening is at hand,
make it bright for us.
Abide with me, O Lord,
for evening has come
and the day is far spent.
Let your strength be made perfect
in my weakness.

This day is quickly gone,
too quickly, like all our days.
The Lord has granted loving-kindness in the day
    time
and in the night season also I will sing God's praise
and make my prayer to the God of my life.
As long as I live will I praise you in this way
and lift up my hands in your Name.
Let my prayer be set forth in your sight as incense
and let the lifting up of my hands
be an evening sacrifice.
Blessed are you, O Lord our God,
you created the change of day to night,

you have delivered us from the dangers of the day,
and brought us again to a time of rest and peace.

Lord,
as we add day to day,
so we add sin to sin.
The just fall seven times a day
and I, an unprofitable servant,
seventy times seven.
But now I turn to you
with sorrow and repentance
and with all my heart.
O God of penitents and Savior of sinners,
evening by evening I will return
and out of the depths of my soul cry to you.
I have sinned, O Lord, I have sinned.
I repent and turn to you for forgiveness.

Lord, have mercy on me,
heal my soul for I have sinned against you.
Have mercy on me, O Lord,
according to your great goodness,
according to the multitude of your mercies
do away my offenses.
Pardon the guilt,
heal the wound,
blot out the stains,
clear away the shame,
let not sin have dominion in my life.
Lord, bring my life out of trouble
and cleanse me from my hidden faults.

Whatever I have done amiss, mercifully pardon.
Do not deal with me according to my sins
nor reward me according to my failures.
Look mercifully on my weaknesses
and for the glory of your all-holy Name
turn from me all those ills and miseries
which by my sins
I most justly have deserved.

Commendation

To my weariness, O Lord,
give rest,
to my exhaustion,
give strength.
Deliver me from the dangers of the night.
Restore me with healthy sleep,
and let me pass through this night without fear.
O Creator of the light,
you neither slumber nor sleep,
guard me this night from all evil,
guard my soul, O Lord.
Let my sleep bring respite.
Preserve me from earthly and evil thoughts.
Lord, you know
my enemies are sleepless;
shelter me under your wings,
awaken me in the morning to a new day
and grant that I may seek you early
for your glory and for your service.

Intercession

I pray for
the created world,
the human race,
all who are in affliction and in prosperity,
in error and in truth,
in sin and in grace,
the whole church throughout the world,
for the clergy and people,
for all who serve in government,
for peace in the world,
for those who work to maintain the community;
for my family,
for those in special need,
for travelers.

Conclusion

*I*nto your hands, O Lord, I commend myself,
my spirit, soul, and body.
You created me and redeemed me
and all my family and those near to me.
Guard my lying down and my rising up,
now and evermore.
Let me remember you this night
and let me wake up to your presence;
let me lie down in peace and take my rest,
for you, Lord, only,
make me dwell in safety. Amen.

Suggestions for Meditation

*M*editation, sometimes called "centering prayer," is a way of turning thoughts to God and "being" more nearly in God's presence. A hotel or motel room, free of the distractions of home or office, can be a very good place to make use of this age-old method of spiritual growth. While meditation can take many forms, the following two methods lend themselves to a traveler's needs.

Before you begin, sit quietly for a moment, pay attention to your breathing, and let your tensions and distractions slip away.

Bible-based meditation

Read a passage from the Bible (such as those on pages 49–80) and then try to enter more deeply into the meaning of the reading with this formula: picture—ponder—pray.

Picture: After your reading, imagine the scene (Jesus giving the sermon on the mount; Jesus teaching beside the lake of Galilee; Jesus teaching the disciples). See the color and shape of the landscape, the people involved, "be there" as nearly as possible. Do you feel the sun beating down? Do you long to splash cool water on your face?

Ponder: Think about the meaning of the words or events. Hear Jesus' words for the first time. What effect do they have on those who are there, listening? What effect do they have on you?

Pray: Ask God's help to let your thoughts bear fruit in your life, to make a difference in your life and those of others. Pray that the passage you have read will influence your life.

Try to hold onto the picture or a few words from the reading as you go about your day or as you are falling asleep at night.

Christian mantras

Buddhists use "mantras" to help them focus their thoughts and enter into a deeper level of spirituality. Christians can use the same technique to center their thoughts and attention on God. One of the oldest such "mantras" is the Jesus Prayer: *Lord Jesus Christ, have mercy on me a sinner.*

Choose one of the mantras below (or make your own) and repeat it over and over, slowly and carefully, coordinating the words with your breathing so that you breathe in as you repeat the phrase and then repeat it again as you breathe out, or use half the phrase as you inhale and half as you exhale. The word "Spirit" in Greek and Hebrew is the same as the word for "breath," so you can think of your breathing as a drawing in of the Holy Spirit to the center of your being.

You might spend five minutes or longer in this way, and then let the mantra remain in your mind during the day or as you fall asleep at night. Come back to it in quiet moments and let it make you aware of God's presence.

Examples of Christian mantras

Lord Jesus Christ, have mercy on me a sinner.
Lord Jesus, have mercy.
Come, Holy Spirit, fill my heart and mind.
Come, Holy Spirit.
Glory to you, Lord God.
Come, Lord Jesus, and be with me this day (night).
Come, Lord Jesus.
Lord, I believe; help my unbelief.
Lord, not my will but yours be done.

In addition, each of the following readings ends with two suggestions for meditation which might be used as mantras.

Readings from the Bible

The following readings center on two themes: Who is God? How have people encountered God in their travels? Each reading is followed by two brief phrases that you might use as "mantras" (see page 45) to help keep the reading and its meaning in your mind.

The vision of God   (Isaiah 6:1–10)

*I*n the year that King Uzziah died, I saw the Lord sitting on a throne, high and lofty; and the hem of his robe filled the temple. Seraphs were in attendance above him; each had six wings: with two they covered their faces, and with two they covered their feet, and with two they flew. And one called to another and said:

> "Holy, holy, holy is the Lord of hosts;
> the whole earth is full of his glory."

The pivots on the thresholds shook at the voices of those who called, and the house filled with smoke. And I said: "Woe is me! I am lost, for I am a man of unclean lips, and I live among a people of unclean lips; yet my eyes have seen the King, the Lord of hosts!"

Then one of the seraphs flew to me, holding a live coal that had been taken from the altar with a pair of tongs. The seraph touched my mouth with it and said: "Now that this has touched your lips, your guilt has departed and your sin is blotted out." Then I heard the voice of the Lord saying, "Whom shall I send, and who will go for us?" And I said, "Here am I; send me!"

For meditation

- *The whole earth is full of his glory.*
- *Here am I; send me!*

God's presence with a traveler
(Genesis 28:10–21)

Jacob left Beer-sheba and went toward Haran. He came to a certain place and stayed there for the night, because the sun had set. Taking one of the stones of the place, he put it under his head and lay down in that place.

And he dreamed that there was a ladder set up on the earth, the top of it reaching to heaven; and the angels of God were ascending and descending on it. And the LORD stood beside him and said, "I am the LORD, the God of Abraham your father and the God of Isaac; the land on which you lie I will give to you and to your offspring; and your offspring shall be like the dust of the earth, and you shall spread abroad to the west and to the east and to the north and to the south; and all the families of the earth shall be blessed in you and in your offspring. Know that I am with you and will keep you wherever you go, and will bring you back to this land; for I will not leave you until I have done what I have promised you."

Then Jacob woke from his sleep and said, "Surely the LORD is in this place—and I did not know it!" And he was afraid, and said, "How awesome is this place! This is none other than the house of God, and this is the gate of heaven."

So Jacob rose early in the morning, and he took the stone that he had put under his head and set it up for a pillar and poured oil on the top of it. He called that place Bethel; but the name of the city was Luz at the first. Then Jacob made a vow, saying, "If God will be with me, and will keep me in this way that I go, and will give me bread to eat and clothing to wear, so that I come again to my father's house in peace, then the LORD shall be my God.

For meditation

❰ *Know that I am with you and will keep you wherever you go.*

❰ *Surely the LORD is in this place.*

God's welcome of strangers   (Ruth 1:1–19)

*I*n the days when the judges ruled, there was a famine in the land, and a certain man of Bethlehem in Judah went to live in the country of Moab, he and his wife and two sons. The name of the man was Elimelech and the name of his wife Naomi, and the names of his two sons were Mahlon and Chilion; they were Ephrathites from Bethlehem in Judah.

They went into the country of Moab and remained there. But Elimelech, the husband of Naomi, died, and she was left with her two sons. These took Moabite wives; the name of the one was Orpah and the name of the other Ruth. When they had lived there about ten years, both Mahlon and Chilion also died, so that the woman was left without her two sons and her husband.

Then she started to return with her daughters-in-law from the country of Moab, for she had heard in the country of Moab that the LORD had considered his people and given them food. So she set out from the place where she had been living, she and her two daughters-in-law, and they went on their way to go back to the land of Judah. But Naomi said to her two daughters-in-law, "Go back each of you to your mother's house. May the LORD deal kindly with you, as you have dealt with the dead and with me. The LORD grant that you may find security, each of you in the house of your husband." Then she kissed them, and they wept aloud.

They said to her, "No, we will return with you to your people."

But Naomi said, "Turn back, my daughters, why will you go with me? Do I still have sons in my womb that they may become your husbands? Turn back, my daughters, go your way, for I am too old to have a husband. Even if I thought there was hope for me, even if I should have a husband tonight and bear sons, would you then wait until they were grown? Would you then refrain from marrying? No, my daughters, it has been far more bitter for me than for you, because the hand of the LORD has turned against me."

Then they wept aloud again. Orpah kissed her mother-in-law, but Ruth clung to her. So she said, "See, your sister-in-law has gone back to her people and to her gods; return after your sister-in-law." But Ruth said,

"Do not press me to leave you
  or to turn back from following you!
Where you go, I will go;
  where you lodge, I will lodge;
your people shall be my people,
  and your God my God.
Where you die, I will die—
  there will I be buried.
May the LORD do thus and so to me,
  and more as well,
if even death parts me from you!"

When Naomi saw that she was determined to go with her, she said no more to her. So the two of them went on until they came to Bethlehem.

For meditation

- *May the LORD deal kindly with you.*
- *Your God shall be my God.*

God's care for us (Isaiah 40:1–11)

Comfort, O comfort my people,
 says your God.
Speak tenderly to Jerusalem,
 and cry to her
that she has served her term,
 that her penalty is paid,
that she has received from the Lord's hand
 double for all her sins.

A voice cries out:
"In the wilderness prepare the way of the LORD,
 make straight in the desert a highway
 for our God.
Every valley shall be lifted up,
 and every mountain and hill be made low;
the uneven ground shall become level,
 and the rough places a plain.
Then the glory of the LORD shall be revealed,
 and all people shall see it together,
 for the mouth of the LORD has spoken."

A voice says, "Cry out!"
 And I said, "What shall I cry?"
All people are grass,
 their constancy is like the flower of the field.

The grass withers, the flower fades,
  when the breath of the LORD blows upon it;
  surely the people are grass.
The grass withers, the flower fades;
  but the word of our God will stand forever.
Get you up to a high mountain,
  O Zion, herald of good tidings;
lift up your voice with strength,
  O Jerusalem, herald of good tidings,
  lift it up, do not fear;
say to the cities of Judah,
  "Here is your God!"
See, the Lord GOD comes with might,
  and his arm rules for him;
his reward is with him,
  and his recompense before him.
He will feed his flock like a shepherd;
  he will gather the lambs in his arms,
and carry them in his bosom,
  and gently lead the mother sheep.

For meditation

  ⤷   *The word of our God will stand forever.*
  ⤷   *He will feed his flock like a shepherd.*

God's call to us   (Isaiah 55)

*H*o, everyone who thirsts, come to the waters;
and you that have no money,
  come, buy and eat!
Come, buy wine and milk
  without money and without price.
Why do you spend your money for that which is
            not bread,
  and your labor for that which does not satisfy?

Listen carefully to me, and eat what is good,
  and delight yourselves in rich food.
Incline your ear, and come to me;
  listen, so that you may live.
I will make with you an everlasting covenant,
  my steadfast, sure love for David.
See, I made him a witness to the peoples,
  a leader and commander for the peoples.
See, you shall call nations that you do not know,
  and nations that do not know you shall run to you,
because of the LORD your God, the Holy One of
            Israel,
  for he has glorified you.

Seek the LORD while he may be found,
  call upon him while he is near;
let the wicked forsake their way,
  and the unrighteous their thoughts;
let them return to the LORD, that he may have
              mercy on them,
  and to our God, for he will abundantly pardon.
For my thoughts are not your thoughts,
  nor are your ways my ways, says the LORD.
For as the heavens are higher than the earth,
  so are my ways higher than your ways
  and my thoughts than your thoughts.

For as the rain and the snow come down from
              heaven,
  and do not return there until they have watered
              the earth,
making it bring forth and sprout,
  giving seed to the sower and bread to the eater,
so shall my word be that goes out from my mouth;
  it shall not return to me empty,
but it shall accomplish that which I purpose,
  and succeed in the thing for which I sent it.

For you shall go out in joy,
    and be led back in peace;
the mountains and the hills before you
    shall burst into song,
    and all the trees of the field shall clap their hands.
Instead of the thorn shall come up the cypress;
    instead of the brier shall come up the myrtle;
    and it shall be to the LORD for a memorial,
        for an everlasting sign that shall not be cut off.

For meditation

🖎   *Listen, so that you may live.*
🖎   *Seek the LORD while he may be found.*

God's concern for justice   (Amos 8:4–12)

*H*ear this, you that trample on the needy,
   and bring to ruin the poor of the land,
saying, "When will the new moon be over
   so that we may sell grain;
and the sabbath,
   so that we may offer wheat for sale?
We will make the ephah small and the shekel great,
   and practice deceit with false balances,
buying the poor for silver
   and the needy for a pair of sandals,
   and selling the sweepings of the wheat."

The LORD has sworn by the pride of Jacob:
Surely I will never forget any of their deeds.
Shall not the land tremble on this account,
   and everyone mourn who lives in it,
and all of it rise like the Nile,
and be tossed about and sink again,
   like the Nile of Egypt?

On that day, says the Lord GOD,
   I will make the sun go down at noon,
   and darken the earth in broad daylight.
I will turn your feasts into mourning,
   and all your songs into lamentation;
I will bring sackcloth on all loins,
   and baldness on every head;

I will make it like the mourning for an only son,
   and the end of it like a bitter day.

The time is surely coming, says the Lord GOD,
   when I will send a famine on the land;
not a famine of bread, or a thirst for water,
   but of hearing the words of the LORD.
They shall wander from sea to sea,
   and from north to east;
they shall run to and fro,
            seeking the word of the LORD,
   but they shall not find it.

For meditation

⁂   *The LORD will never forget their deeds.*

⁂   *They shall seek the word of the LORD, but not find it.*

The beatitudes   (Matthew 5:1–12)

*W*hen Jesus saw the crowds, he went up the mountain; and after he sat down, his disciples came to him. Then he began to speak, and taught them, saying:

"Blessed are the poor in spirit, for theirs is the kingdom of heaven.

"Blessed are those who mourn, for they will be comforted.

"Blessed are the meek, for they will inherit the earth.

"Blessed are those who hunger and thirst for righteousness, for they will be filled.

"Blessed are the merciful, for they will receive mercy.

"Blessed are the pure in heart, for they will see God.

"Blessed are the peacemakers, for they will be called children of God.

"Blessed are those who are persecuted for righteousness' sake, for theirs is the kingdom of heaven.

"Blessed are you when people revile you and persecute you and utter all kinds of evil against you falsely on my account. Rejoice and be glad, for your reward is great in heaven, for in the same way they persecuted the prophets who were before you."

For meditation

- ᕲ *His disciples came to him.*
- ᕲ *Blessed are the peacemakers.*

Do not worry (Matthew 6:24–34)

*J*esus said, "No one can serve two masters; for a slave will either hate the one and love the other, or be devoted to the one and despise the other. You cannot serve God and wealth.

"Therefore I tell you, do not worry about your life, what you will eat or what you will drink, or about your body, what you will wear. Is not life more than food, and the body more than clothing? Look at the birds of the air; they neither sow nor reap nor gather into barns, and yet your heavenly Father feeds them. Are you not of more value than they? And can any of you by worrying add a single hour to your span of life? And why do you worry about clothing?

"Consider the lilies of the field, how they grow; they neither toil nor spin, yet I tell you, even Solomon in all his glory was not clothed like one of these. But if God so clothes the grass of the field, which is alive today and tomorrow is thrown into the oven, will he not much more clothe you—you of little faith?

"Therefore do not worry, saying, 'What will we eat?' or 'What will we drink?' or 'What will we wear?' For it is the Gentiles who strive for all these things; and indeed your heavenly Father knows that you need all these things. But strive first for the kingdom of God and his righteousness, and all these things will be given to you as well.

"So do not worry about tomorrow, for tomorrow will bring worries of its own. Today's trouble is enough for today."

For meditation

- *You cannot serve God and wealth.*
- *Strive first for the kingdom.*

The good Samaritan and a traveler
(Luke 10:25–37)

A lawyer stood up to test Jesus. "Teacher," he said, "what must I do to inherit eternal life?" He said to him, "What is written in the law? What do you read there?" He answered, "You shall love the Lord your God with all your heart, and with all your soul, and with all your strength, and with all your mind; and your neighbor as yourself." And he said to him, "You have given the right answer; do this, and you will live."

But wanting to justify himself, he asked Jesus, "And who is my neighbor?" Jesus replied, "A man was going down from Jerusalem to Jericho, and fell into the hands of robbers, who stripped him, beat him, and went away, leaving him half dead. Now by chance a priest was going down that road; and when he saw him, he passed by on the other side. So likewise a Levite, when he came to the place and saw him, passed by on the other side. But a Samaritan while traveling came near him; and when he saw him, he was moved with pity. He went to him and bandaged his wounds, having poured oil and wine on them. Then he put him on his own animal, brought him to an inn, and took care of him.

"The next day he took out two denarii, gave them to the innkeeper, and said, 'Take care of him; and when I come back, I will repay you whatever more you spend.' Which of these three, do you think, was a neighbor to the man who fell into the hands of the robbers?" He said, "The one who showed him mercy." Jesus said to him, "Go and do likewise."

For meditation

- *Who is my neighbor?*
- *Go and do likewise.*

Jesus walks with two disciples (Luke 24:13–35)

$\mathcal{N}$ow on that same day two of them were going to a village called Emmaus, about seven miles from Jerusalem, and talking with each other about all these things that had happened. While they were talking and discussing, Jesus himself came near and went with them, but their eyes were kept from recognizing him. And he said to them, "What are you discussing with each other while you walk along?"

They stood still, looking sad. Then one of them, whose name was Cleopas, answered him, "Are you the only stranger in Jerusalem who does not know the things that have taken place there in these days?" He asked them, "What things?" They replied, "The things about Jesus of Nazareth, who was a prophet mighty in deed and word before God and all the people, and how our chief priests and leaders handed him over to be condemned to death and crucified him. But we had hoped that he was the one to redeem Israel.

"Yes, and besides all this, it is now the third day since these things took place. Moreover, some women of our group astounded us. They were at the tomb early this morning, and when they did not find his body there, they came back and told us that they had indeed seen a vision of angels who said that he was alive. Some of those who were with us went to the tomb and found it just as the women had said; but they did not see him."

Then he said to them, "Oh, how foolish you are, and how slow of heart to believe all that the prophets have declared! Was it not necessary that the Messiah should suffer these things and then enter into his glory?" Then beginning with Moses and all the prophets, he interpreted to them the things about himself in all the scriptures.

As they came near the village to which they were going, he walked ahead as if he were going on. But they urged him strongly, saying, "Stay with us, because it is almost evening and the day is now nearly over." So he went in to stay with them. When he was at the table with them, he took bread, blessed and broke it, and gave it to them. Then their eyes were opened, and they recognized him; and he vanished from their sight.

They said to each other, "Were not our hearts burning within us while he was talking to us on the road, while he was opening the scriptures to us?" That same hour they got up and returned to Jerusalem; and they found the eleven and their companions gathered together. They were saying, "The Lord has risen indeed, and he has appeared to Simon!" Then they told what had happened on the road, and how he had been made known to them in the breaking of the bread.

For meditation

- *Necessary that the Messiah should suffer . . .*
- *The Lord has risen indeed.*

The meaning of love   (1 Corinthians 13)

*I*f I speak in the tongues of mortals and of angels, but do not have love, I am a noisy gong or a clanging cymbal. And if I have prophetic powers, and understand all mysteries and all knowledge, and if I have all faith, so as to remove mountains, but do not have love, I am nothing. If I give away all my possessions, and if I hand over my body so that I may boast, but do not have love, I gain nothing.

Love is patient; love is kind; love is not envious or boastful or arrogant or rude. It does not insist on its own way; it is not irritable or resentful; it does not rejoice in wrongdoing, but rejoices in the truth. It bears all things, believes all things, hopes all things, endures all things.

Love never ends. But as for prophecies, they will come to an end; as for tongues, they will cease; as for knowledge, it will come to an end. For we know only in part, and we prophesy only in part; but when the complete comes, the partial will come to an end.

When I was a child, I spoke like a child, I thought like a child, I reasoned like a child; when I became an adult, I put an end to childish ways. For now we see in a mirror, dimly, but then we will see face to face. Now I know only in part; then I will know fully, even as I have been fully known. And now faith, hope, and love abide, these three; and the greatest of these is love.

For meditation

- *If I have all faith, so as to remove mountains, but do not have love, I am nothing.*
- *Love never ends.*

The cosmic Christ   (Colossians 1:15–20)

*H*e is the image of the invisible God, the
firstborn of all creation; for in him all things in
heaven and on earth were created, things visible
and invisible, whether thrones or dominions or
rulers or powers—all things have been created
through him and for him. He himself is before all
things, and in him all things hold together. He is
the head of the body, the church; he is the
beginning, the firstborn from the dead, so that he
might come to have first place in everything. For
in him all the fullness of God was pleased to
dwell, and through him God was pleased to
reconcile to himself all things, whether on earth
or in heaven, by making peace through the blood
of his cross.

For meditation

- ⤷   *He is the beginning.*
- ⤷   *Peace through the blood of his cross . . .*

The meaning of faith   (Hebrews 11)

$\mathcal{N}$ow faith is the assurance of things hoped for, the conviction of things not seen. Indeed, by faith our ancestors received approval. By faith we understand that the worlds were prepared by the word of God, so that what is seen was made from things that are not visible.

By faith Abel offered to God a more acceptable sacrifice than Cain's. Through this he received approval as righteous, God himself giving approval to his gifts; he died, but through his faith he still speaks. By faith Enoch was taken so that he did not experience death; and "he was not found, because God had taken him." For it was attested before he was taken away that "he had pleased God." And without faith it is impossible to please God, for whoever would approach him must believe that he exists and that he rewards those who seek him. By faith Noah, warned by God about events as yet unseen, respected the warning and built an ark to save his household; by this he condemned the world and became an heir to the righteousness that is in accordance with faith.

By faith Abraham obeyed when he was called to set out for a place that he was to receive as an inheritance; and he set out, not knowing where he was going. By faith he stayed for a time in the land he had been promised, as in a foreign land, living in tents, as did Isaac and Jacob, who were heirs with him of the same promise.

For he looked forward to the city that has foundations, whose architect and builder is God. By faith he received power of procreation, even though he was too old—and Sarah herself was barren—because he considered him faithful who had promised. Therefore from one person, and this one as good as dead, descendants were born, "as many as the stars of heaven and as the innumerable grains of sand by the seashore."

All of these died in faith without having received the promises, but from a distance they saw and greeted them. They confessed that they were strangers and foreigners on the earth, for people who speak in this way make it clear that they are seeking a homeland. If they had been thinking of the land that they had left behind, they would have had opportunity to return. But as it is, they desire a better country, that is, a heavenly one.

Therefore God is not ashamed to be called their God; indeed, he has prepared a city for them.

By faith Abraham, when put to the test, offered up Isaac. He who had received the promises was ready to offer up his only son, of whom he had been told, "It is through Isaac that descendants shall be named for you." He considered the fact that God is able even to raise someone from the dead—and figuratively speaking, he did receive him back. By faith Isaac invoked blessings for the future on Jacob and Esau. By faith Jacob, when dying, blessed each of the sons of Joseph, "bowing in worship over the top of his staff." By faith Joseph, at the end of his life, made mention of the exodus of the Israelites and gave instructions about his burial.

By faith Moses was hidden by his parents for three months after his birth, because they saw that the child was beautiful; and they were not afraid of the king's edict. By faith Moses, when he was grown up, refused to be called a son of Pharaoh's daughter, choosing rather to share ill-treatment with the people of God than to enjoy the fleeting pleasures of sin. He considered abuse suffered for the Christ to be greater wealth than the treasures of Egypt, for he was looking ahead to the reward. By faith he left Egypt, unafraid of the king's anger; for he persevered as though he saw him who is invisible. By faith he kept the Passover and the sprinkling of blood, so that the destroyer of the firstborn would not touch the firstborn of Israel.

By faith the people passed through the Red Sea as if it were dry land, but when the Egyptians attempted to do so they were drowned. By faith the walls of Jericho fell after they had been encircled for seven days. By faith Rahab the prostitute did not perish with those who were disobedient, because she had received the spies in peace.

And what more should I say? For time would fail me to tell of Gideon, Barak, Samson, Jephthah, of David and Samuel and the prophets—who through faith conquered kingdoms, administered justice, obtained promises, shut the mouths of lions, quenched raging fire, escaped the edge of the sword, won strength out of weakness, became mighty in war, put foreign armies to flight. Women received their dead by resurrection. Others were tortured, refusing to accept release, in order to obtain a better resurrection. Others suffered mocking and flogging, and even chains and imprisonment. They were stoned to death, they were sawn in two, they were killed by the sword; they went about in skins of sheep and goats, destitute, persecuted, tormented—of whom the world was not worthy. They wandered in deserts and mountains, and in caves and holes in the ground.

Yet all these, though they were commended for their faith, did not receive what was promised, since God had provided something better so that they would not, apart from us, be made perfect.

For meditation

- *Without faith it is impossible to please God.*
- *Faith is the assurance of things hoped for, the conviction of things not seen.*

The vision of heaven   (Revelation 21:1–7)

I saw a new heaven and a new earth; for the first
heaven and the first earth had passed away, and
the sea was no more. And I saw the holy city, the
new Jerusalem, coming down out of heaven from
God, prepared as a bride adorned for her
husband. And I heard a loud voice from the
throne saying,

"See, the home of God is among mortals.
He will dwell with them as their God;
they will be his peoples,
and God himself will be with them;
he will wipe every tear from their eyes.
Death will be no more;
mourning and crying and pain will be no more,
for the first things have passed away."

And the one who was seated on the throne said,
"See, I am making all things new." Also he said,
"Write this, for these words are trustworthy and
true." Then he said to me, "It is done! I am the

Alpha and the Omega, the beginning and the end. To the thirsty I will give water as a gift from the spring of the water of life. Those who conquer will inherit these things, and I will be their God and they will be my children."

For meditation

- ✎ *I saw a new heaven and a new earth.*
- ✎ *I am making all things new.*
- ✎ *I am the Alpha and the Omega, the beginning and the end.*

Readings from other Sources

Passing through the world
(The Epistle to Diognetus, c. 124 A.D.)

Christians are indistinguishable from others either by nationality, language, or customs. They do not inhabit separate cities of their own, or speak a strange dialect, or follow some outlandish way of life. Their teaching is not based on dreams inspired by the curiosity of human beings. Unlike some other people, they champion no purely human doctrine. With regard to dress, food, and manner of life in general, they follow the customs of whatever city they happen to be living in, whether it is Greek or foreign.

And yet there is something extraordinary about their lives. They live in their own countries as though they were only passing through. They play their full role as citizens, but labor under all the disabilities of aliens. Any country can be their homeland, but for them their homeland, wherever it may be, is a foreign country. They live in the flesh, but they are not governed by the desires of the flesh. They pass their days upon earth, but they are citizens of heaven. Obedient to the laws, they yet live on a level that transcends the law.

To speak in general terms we may say that the Christian is to the world what the soul is to the body. As the soul is present in every part of the body, while remaining distinct from it, so Christians are found in all the cities of the world, but cannot be identified with the world. It is by the soul, enclosed within the body, that the body is held together, and similarly it is by these Christians, detained in the world as in a prison, that the world is held together.

For meditation

- *Their homeland is a foreign country.*
- *Citizens of heaven . . .*

Lord, you know me
(St. Augustine of Hippo, 354–430)

*L*ord, you know me. Let me know you. Let me come to know you even as I am known. You are the strength of my soul; enter it and make it a place suitable for your dwelling, a possession "without spot or blemish." This is my hope and the reason I speak. In this hope I rejoice, when I rejoice rightly.

As for the other things of this life, the less they deserve tears, the more likely will they be lamented; and the more they deserve tears, the less likely will people sorrow for them. "For behold, you have loved the truth, because the one who does what is true enters into the light." I wish to do this truth before you alone by praising you and before a multitude of witnesses by writing of you.

O Lord, the depths of my conscience lie exposed before your eyes. Could anything remain hidden in me, even though I did not want to confess it to you? In that case I would only be hiding you from myself, not myself from you. But now my sighs are sufficient evidence that I am displeased with myself; that you are my light and the source of my joy; that you are loved and desired. I am thoroughly ashamed of myself; I have renounced myself and chosen you, recognizing that I can please neither you nor myself unless you enable me to do so.

Whoever I may be, Lord, I lie exposed to your scrutiny. I have already told of the profit I gain when I confess to you. And I do not make my confession with bodily words, bodily speech, but with the words of my soul and the cry of my mind which you hear and understand. When I am wicked, my confession to you is an expression of displeasure with myself. But when I do good, it consists in not attributing this goodness to myself. "For you, O Lord, bless the just," but first "you justify the wicked." And so I make my confession before you in silence, and yet not in silence. My voice is silent, but my heart cries out.

You, O Lord, are my judge. For "though no one knows a person's innermost self except the spirit within," yet there is something within which even one's own spirit does not know. But you know all of a person, for you have made us all. As for me, I despise myself in your sight, knowing that I am but dust and ashes; yet I know something of you that I do not know of myself.

True, "we see now indistinctly as in a mirror, but not yet face to face." Therefore, so long as I am in exile from you, I am more present to myself than to you. Yet I do know that you cannot be overcome, while I am uncertain which temptations I can resist and which I cannot. Nevertheless, I have hope, because "you are faithful and do not allow us to be tempted beyond our endurance, but along with the temptation you give us the means to withstand it."

I will confess, therefore, what I know of myself, and also what I do not know. The knowledge that I have of myself, I possess because you have enlightened me; while the knowledge of myself that I do not yet possess will not be mine until my darkness shall be made as the noonday sun before your face.

For meditation

- *Lord, I lie exposed to your scrutiny.*
- *Lord, let me know you.*

God's love   (Julian of Norwich, 1342–after 1413)

*O*ur Lord showed me a little thing, the size of a hazelnut, in the palm of his hand; and it was as round as a ball. I looked at it with the eye of my understanding, and thought, "What may this be?" And it was generally answered thus, "It is all that is made." I marveled how it might last, for I thought it might suddenly have fallen to nothing for littleness. And I was answered in my understanding, "It lasts, and ever shall last, because God loves it." And so all things have their being by the love of God.

And from that time that it was shown, I desired often to know what was our Lord's meaning. And I was answered in spiritual understanding, "Would you understand your Lord's meaning? Understand it well: Love was God's meaning. Who showed it to you? Love. What did he show you? Love. Why did God show it to you? For love." Thus did I learn that Love was our Lord's meaning.

And I saw full surely in this and in all, that before God made us God loved us; which love was never slackened nor ever shall be. And in this love God has done all that God made; and in this love God has made all things profitable to us; and in this love our life is everlasting. In our making we had beginning; for the love in which God made us was in God from without beginning; in which love we have our beginning. And all this shall we see in God without end. Which may Jesus grant us.

For meditation

- Before God made us God loved us.
- Love was God's meaning.

Strangers and pilgrims
(Martin Luther, 1483–1546)

*W*e should look upon this life as a stranger and pilgrim looks upon a land in which he is a stranger and a guest. Strangers cannot say, Here is my homeland, for they are not at home there. Pilgrims do not think of remaining in the land to which they make their pilgrimage or in the inn in which they spend the night, but their thoughts and hearts are directed elsewhere. They feed in the inn and rest, and then continue their journey home.

Therefore conduct yourselves as guests and strangers in this strange land and strange inn, and take nothing from it but food and drink, clothing and shoes, and what you need for your night's rest, and keep your thoughts on your homeland where you are citizens.

We must note this carefully. We must not seek to build for ourselves eternal life here in this world and pursue it and cleave to it as if it were our greatest treasure and heavenly kingdom, as if we wished to exploit the Lord Christ and the Gospel and achieve wealth and power through him. No, but because we have to live on earth, and as long as it is God's will, we should eat, drink, woo, plant, build, and have house and home and what God grants, and use these things as guests and strangers in a strange land, who know they must leave them behind and depart this strange land and evil, unsafe inn, bound for our true homeland where there is nothing but security, peace, rest, and joy for evermore.

For meditation

- ᔓ *Look on this life as a stranger.*
- ᔓ *Keep your thoughts on your homeland.*

True riches   (John Donne, 1571/2–1631)

*A*ll of us may find in ourselves, that we have
done some sins which we would not have done if
we had not been so rich, for there is a cost for
most sins. Our wealth gave us a confidence that
that fault would not be looked into, or that it
would be bought out if it were. Some sins we
have done because we are rich, but many more
because we wished to be rich. And this is a
spiritual harm that riches do their owners.

The rich merchant at sea is afraid that every
fisherman is a pirate, but the fisherman fears not
the merchant. It is true the poor man's brow
sweats without; the rich man's heart bleeds
within. And the poor man can sooner wipe his
face than the rich man his heart. Sum up the
diseases that the ministry of riches imprints in the
body, the assault that malice provoked by riches
lays to the fortune, the sins that confidence in our
riches heaps on our souls, and we shall see that
though riches be reserved to their owners, yet it
is to their harm.

The blessedness of having studied and learned
and practiced the knowledge of God's purpose
shall endure for ever. When you shall turn from

Other Prayers

In Praise of God

O burning Mountain, O chosen Sun,
  O perfect Moon, O fathomless Well,
O unattainable Height, O Clearness beyond measure,
  O Wisdom without end, O Mercy without limit,
O Strength beyond resistance, O Crown beyond
                 all majesty:
The humblest thing you created sings your praise.

(Mechtilde of Magdeburg, 13ᵗʰ century)

For the Peace of God's presence

*G*od of peace,
let us your people know,
that at the heart of turbulence
there is an inner calm that comes
from faith in you.
Keep us from being content with things as they are,
that from this central peace
there may come a creative compassion,
a thirst for justice,
and a willingness to give of ourselves
in the Spirit of Christ. Amen.

(A New Zealand Prayer Book)

For Joy in God's Creation

O heavenly Father, you have filled the world
with beauty: Open our eyes to behold your
gracious hand in all your works; that, rejoicing in
your whole creation, we may learn to serve
you with gladness; for the sake of him through
whom all things were made, your Son Jesus
Christ our Lord. Amen.

For Travelers

*L*ord of the universe, the whole world is full of
your glory. Wherever I go, you are near to me. "If
I take up the wings of the morning, and dwell on
the ocean's farthest shore, even there your hand
will lead me, your right hand will hold me." You
have always been a light to my path. Now that I
begin a new journey, I turn to you in confidence
and trust. Protect me from the perils of the way.
May I go forth in health and safely reach my
destination. May this journey not be in vain; let its
purpose be fulfilled; let me return in contentment
to those I love. Then shall I know your blessing in
all my travels. Amen.

(Traditional Jewish prayer, adapted from *Gates of the House:
The New Union Prayerbook*)

O God, you called Abraham and Sarah to leave
their home and protected them in all their
wanderings: Grant those who travel now by land,
sea, or air, a prosperous journey, a time of peace,
and a safe arrival at their journey's end. Be to
them a shadow in the heat, a refuge in the
tempest, a protection in adversity, and grant that
when life's pilgrimage is over they may arrive at
the heavenly country; through Jesus Christ our
Lord. Amen.

O God, our heavenly Father, whose glory fills the
whole creation, and whose presence we find
wherever we go: Preserve those who travel;
surround them with your loving care; protect
them from every danger; and bring them in safety
to their journey's end; through Jesus Christ our
Lord. Amen.

*A*lmighty God, whose kingdom is for the poor in
spirit, and whose best provision for your chosen
people is a tent and a pilgrim's staff; grant that
we look not for permanence in the work of
human hands, nor seek safety except in the
company of that Wayfarer who had nowhere to
lay his head, even your Son Jesus Christ our Lord.
Amen.

(Church Mission Society, *More Prayers for Sunday*)

For our Country

*A*lmighty God, who hast given us this good land for our heritage: We humbly beseech thee that we may always prove ourselves a people mindful of thy favor and glad to do thy will. Bless our land with honorable industry, sound learning, and pure manners. Save us from violence, discord, and confusion; from pride and arrogance, and from every evil way. Defend our liberties, and fashion into one united people the multitudes brought hither out of many kindreds and tongues. Endue with the spirit of wisdom those to whom in thy Name we entrust the authority of government, that there may be justice and peace at home, and that, through obedience to thy law, we may show forth thy praise among the nations of the earth. In the time of prosperity, fill our hearts with thankfulness, and in the day of trouble, suffer not our trust in thee to fail; all which we ask through Jesus Christ our Lord. Amen.

For the President of the United States and all in Civil Authority

O Lord our Governor, whose glory is in all the world: We commend this nation to your merciful care, that, being guided by your Providence, we may dwell secure in your peace. Grant to the President of the United States, the members of Congress and the courts, the Governor of this State (*or* Commonwealth), and to all in authority, wisdom and strength to know and to do your will. Fill them with the love of truth and righteousness, and make them ever mindful of their calling to serve this people in your fear; through Jesus Christ our Lord, who lives and reigns with you and the Holy Spirit, one God, world without end. Amen.

For People of Every Kind

O God, the creator and preserver of all the human race, we humbly pray for all people everywhere, that you would be pleased to make your ways known to them, your saving health to all nations. More especially we pray for your holy Church universal; that it may be so guided and governed by your good Spirit, that all who profess and call themselves Christians may be led into the way of truth, and hold the faith in unity of spirit, in the bond of peace, and in righteousness of life. Finally, we commend to your goodness all those who are in any way afflicted or distressed, in mind, body, or estate; [especially those for whom our prayers are desired]; that it may please you to comfort and relieve them according to their various needs, giving them patience in their sufferings, and a happy issue out of all their afflictions. And this we beg for Jesus Christ's sake. Amen.

For the Human Family

O God, you made us in your own image and redeemed us through Jesus your Son: Look with compassion on the whole human family; take away the arrogance and hatred which infect our hearts; break down the walls that separate us; unite us in bonds of love; and work through our struggle and confusion to accomplish your purposes on earth; that, in your good time, all nations and races may serve you in harmony around your heavenly throne; through Jesus Christ our Lord. Amen.

For Peace

*E*ternal God, in whose perfect kingdom no sword is drawn but the sword of righteousness, no strength known but the strength of love: So mightily spread abroad your Spirit, that all peoples may be gathered under the banner of the Prince of Peace, as children of one Father; to whom be dominion and glory, now and for ever. Amen.

For Peace Among the Nations

*A*lmighty God our heavenly Father, guide the nations of the world into the way of justice and truth, and establish among them that peace which is the fruit of righteousness, that they may become the kingdom of our Lord and Savior Jesus Christ. Amen.

For our Enemies

O God, the Father of all, whose Son commanded us to love our enemies: Lead them and us from prejudice to truth; deliver them and us from hatred, cruelty, and revenge; and in your good time enable us all to stand reconciled before you; through Jesus Christ our Lord. Amen.

For the Church

*G*racious Father, we pray for thy holy Catholic Church. Fill it with all truth, in all truth with all peace. Where it is corrupt, purify it; where it is in error, direct it; where in any thing it is amiss, reform it. Where it is right, strengthen it; where it is in want, provide for it; where it is divided, reunite it; for the sake of Jesus Christ thy Son our Savior. Amen.

For the Mission of the Church

*E*verliving God, whose will it is that all should come to you through your Son Jesus Christ: Inspire our witness to him, that all may know the power of his forgiveness and the hope of his resurrection; who lives and reigns with you and the Holy Spirit, one God, now and for ever. Amen.

For those we Love

*A*lmighty God, we entrust all who are dear to us to thy never-failing care and love, for this life and the life to come, knowing that thou art doing for them better things than we can desire or pray for; through Jesus Christ our Lord. Amen.

For those from whom we are Separated

O God, whose loving care for us reaches to the most distant areas of the world: We ask you to watch over and bless those we love (*especially* _____) who are separated from us now. Defend them from all dangers of soul and body; and grant that both they and we, drawing nearer to you, may be bound together by your love in the communion of the Holy Spirit and in the fellowship of the saints; through Jesus Christ our Lord. Amen.

For a Birthday

*W*atch over your servant, Lord, as *her* days increase; bless and guide *her* wherever *she* may be. Strengthen *her* when *she* stands; comfort *her* when discouraged or sorrowful; raise *her* up if *she* falls; and in *her* heart may your peace which passes understanding abide all the days of *her* life; through Jesus Christ our Lord. Amen.

O God, our times are in your hand: Look with favor, we pray, on your servant N. as *he* begins another year. Grant that *he* may grow in wisdom and grace, and strengthen *his* trust in your goodness all the days of *his* life; through Jesus Christ our Lord. Amen.

For the Anniversary of a Marriage

*G*racious God, we remember with thankfulness the vows of love and commitment to you and to each other in marriage made by _____ on this day. We pray for your continued blessing and we pray that _____ may learn from both their joys and sorrows and discover constantly new riches in their life together in you. We ask this in the name of Jesus Christ our Lord. Amen.

(Adapted from *The Book of Alternative Services* of the Anglican Church of Canada)

For a Sick Person

*H*eavenly Father, giver of life and health and strength: Comfort and relieve your servant *N.* and guide those who minister to *her* of your healing gifts; grant *her* confidence in your loving care and recovery of health and strength in your service; through Jesus Christ our Lord. Amen.

For the Departed

*R*emember your servant *N.*, Lord, according to the favor you have shown your people, and grant that having opened to *him* the gates of everlasting life, *he* may go from strength to strength in the life of perfect service in your heavenly kingdom; through Jesus Christ our Lord. Amen.

For a Person in Trouble or Bereavement

O merciful Father, you have taught us in your holy Word that you do not willingly afflict or grieve your children: Look with pity on the sorrows of your servant for whom our prayers are offered. Remember *her*, O Lord, in mercy, nourish *her* soul with patience, comfort *her* with a sense of your goodness, lift up your countenance upon *her*, and give *her* peace; through Jesus Christ our Lord. Amen.

For the Victims of Addiction

O blessed Lord, you ministered to all who came to you: Look with compassion upon all who through addiction have lost their health and freedom. Restore to them the assurance of your unfailing mercy; remove from them the fears that beset them; strengthen them in the work of their recovery; and to those who care for them, give patient understanding and persevering love. Amen.

For Guidance

*D*irect us, O Lord, in all our doings with your most gracious favor, and further us with your continual help; that in all our works begun, continued, and ended in you, we may glorify your holy Name, and finally, by your mercy, obtain everlasting life; through Jesus Christ our Lord. Amen.

O God, by whom the meek are guided in judgment, and light rises up in darkness for the godly: Grant us, in all our doubts and uncertainties, the grace to ask what you would have us do, that the Spirit of wisdom may save us from all false choices, and that in your light we may see light, and in your straight path may not stumble; through Jesus Christ our Lord. Amen.

For Quiet Confidence

O God of peace, you have taught us that in
returning and rest we shall be saved, in quietness
and in confidence shall be our strength: By the
might of your Spirit lift us, we pray, to your
presence, where we may be still and know that
you are God; through Jesus Christ our Lord.
Amen.

For Protection

*A*ssist us mercifully, O Lord, in these our
supplications and prayers, and dispose the way of
your servants towards the attainment of
everlasting salvation; that, among all the changes
and chances of this mortal life, they may ever be
defended by your gracious and ready help;
through Jesus Christ our Lord. Amen.

A Prayer of Self-Dedication

*A*lmighty and eternal God, so draw our hearts to
you, so guide our minds, so fill our imaginations,
so control our wills, that we may be wholly
yours, utterly dedicated to you; and then use us,
we pray, as you will, and always to your glory
and the welfare of your people; through our Lord
and Savior Jesus Christ. Amen.

For the Good Use of Leisure Time

O God,
you rested the seventh day and are still at work;
in the course of this busy life
give us times of refreshment and peace,
and grant that we may so use our leisure
to rebuild our bodies and renew our minds,
that our spirits may be opened
to the goodness of your creation.

A Prayer attributed to St. Francis

*L*ord, make us instruments of your peace. Where
there is hatred, let us sow love; where there is
injury, pardon; where there is discord, union;
where there is doubt, faith; where there is
despair, hope; where there is darkness, light;
where there is sadness, joy. Grant that we may
not so much seek to be consoled as to console; to
be understood as to understand; to be loved as to
love. For it is in giving that we receive; it is in
pardoning that we are pardoned; and it is in
dying that we are born to eternal life. Amen.

A Thanksgiving

*O*ur Lord God, we thank you
for all your blessings,
for life and health,
for laughter and fun,
for all our powers of mind and body,
for our homes and the love of dear ones,
for the richness and variety of this world,
for everything that is good and beautiful and true.
But above all we thank you for giving your Son
to be our Savior and Friend.
May we always find our true happiness
in pleasing you and helping others
to know you and love you,
for Jesus Christ's sake. Amen.

> (Adapted from *The Book of Alternative Services* of the
> Anglican Church of Canada)

In the Evening

O Lord, support us all the day long, until the
shadows lengthen, and the evening comes, and
the busy world is hushed, and the fever of life is
over, and our work is done. Then in your mercy,
grant us a safe lodging, and a holy rest, and peace
at the last. Amen.

In the Evening

*L*ord,
it is night.

The night is for stillness.
Let us be still in the presence of God.

It is night after a long day.
What has been done has been done;
what has not been done has not been done;
let it be.

The night is dark.
Let our fears of the darkness of the world
and of our own lives
rest in you.

The night is quiet.
Let the quietness of your peace enfold us,
all dear to us,
and all who have no peace.

The night heralds the dawn.
Let us look expectantly to a new day,
new joys,
new possibilities.

In your name we pray.
Amen.

(A New Zealand Prayer Book)

For the Answering of Prayer

*A*lmighty God, you have promised to hear the petitions of those who ask in your Son's Name: We beseech you mercifully to incline your ear to us who have now made our prayers and supplications to you; and grant that those things which we have faithfully asked according to your will, may effectually be obtained, to the relief of our necessity, and to the setting forth of your glory; through Jesus Christ our Lord. Amen.

On Sunday

O God our King, by the resurrection of your Son Jesus Christ on the first day of the week, you conquered sin, put death to flight, and gave us the hope of everlasting life: Redeem all our days by this victory; forgive our sins, banish our fears, make us bold to praise you and to do your will; and steel us to wait for the consummation of your kingdom on the last great Day; through the same Jesus Christ our Lord. Amen.

Grace at Meals

*G*ive us grateful hearts, O God our Creator, for all your mercies, and make us mindful of the needs of others; through Jesus Christ our Lord. Amen.

or this

*B*less, O Lord, these gifts to our use and us to your service; for Christ's sake. Amen.

or this

*B*lessed are you, O Lord God, King of the Universe, for you give us food to sustain our lives and make our hearts glad; through Jesus Christ our Lord. Amen.

A Thanksgiving at the
End of a Journey

A Thanksgiving at the End of a Journey

After returning home, these prayers may be said with family and/or friends, a Bible or prayer group, or as part of a weekday service at church.

Give thanks to the LORD, for he is good,
   and his mercy endures for ever.

O God whose mercies cannot be numbered and whose goodness passes all our understanding; I give you thanks for the opportunity to travel in your world and among your people, and for bringing me safely home again; grant me always to remember your guiding hand wherever I may be and to trust in your continuing care for me; through Jesus Christ our Lord. Amen.

Psalm 107 (1–8)

Give thanks to the LORD, for he is good, *
  and his mercy endures for ever.

Let all those whom the LORD has redeemed proclaim *
  that he redeemed them from the hand of the foe.

He gathered them out of the lands; *
from the east and from the west,
  from the north and from the south.

Some wandered in desert wastes; *
  they found no way to a city where they might
      dwell.

They were hungry and thirsty; *
  their spirits languished within them.

Then they cried to the LORD in their trouble, *
  and he delivered them from their distress.

He put their feet on a straight path *
  to go to a city where they might dwell.

Let them give thanks to the LORD for his mercy *
  and the wonders he does for his children.

Give thanks to the LORD, for he is good,
  and his mercy endures for ever.

Lord, have mercy.
   Christ, have mercy.
Lord, have mercy.

Our Father, who art in heaven,
   hallowed be thy Name,
   thy kingdom come,
   thy will be done,
      on earth as it is in heaven.
Give us this day our daily bread.
And forgive us our trespasses,
   as we forgive those
      who trespass against us.
And lead us not into temptation,
   but deliver us from evil.
For thine is the kingdom,
   and the power, and the glory,
   for ever and ever. Amen.

or this

Our Father in heaven,
   hallowed be your Name,
   your kingdom come,
   your will be done,
      on earth as in heaven.

Give us today our daily bread.
Forgive us our sins
   as we forgive those
     who sin against us.
Save us from the time of trial,
   and deliver us from evil.
For the kingdom, the power,
   and the glory are yours,
   now and for ever. Amen.

*T*each us your ways, O Lord,
   and we will walk in your truth.
Happy are those whose way is blameless,
   who walk in the law of the Lord.
In returning and rest you will be saved;
   in quietness and confidence shall be your hope.
Whether we are at home or away,
   we make it our aim to please the Lord.
From the rising of the sun to its going down
   let the Name of the Lord be praised.
The Lord is high above all nations,
   and his glory above the heavens.

*M*y servant David shall be king over them; and
they shall all have one shepherd. They shall
follow my ordinances and be careful to observe
my statutes. They shall live in the land that I gave

to my servant Jacob, in which your ancestors lived; they and their children and their children's children shall live there forever; and my servant David shall be their prince forever.

I will make a covenant of peace with them; it shall be an everlasting covenant with them; and I will bless them and multiply them, and will set my sanctuary among them forevermore. My dwelling place shall be with them; and I will be their God, and they shall be my people. Then the nations shall know that I the LORD sanctify Israel, when my sanctuary is among them forevermore. *(Ezekiel 37:24–28)*

*Y*ou have taught us, Lord God, that we are strangers and pilgrims on this earth and that you have prepared a place for us in your eternal home; make us so mindful of that calling that we may seek to shape our earthly homes in the likeness of that eternal dwelling; through Jesus Christ our Lord. Amen.

*M*ay the Lord watch over my going out and my coming in,
from this time forth for evermore. Amen.